© Copyright 2021 - All rights reserved.

You may not reproduce, duplicate, or send the contents of this book without direct written permission from the author. You cannot hereby despite any circumstance blame the publisher or hold him or her to legal responsibility for any reparation, compensations, or monetary forfeiture owing to the information included herein, either directly or indirectly.

Legal Notice: This book has copyright protection. You can use the book for personal purposes. You should not sell, use, alter, distribute, quote, take excerpts, or paraphrase in part or whole the material contained in this book without obtaining the permission of the author first.

Disclaimer Notice: You must take note that the information in this document is for casual reading and entertainment purposes only.
We have made every attempt to provide accurate, up-to-date, and reliable information. We do not express or imply guarantees of any kind. The persons who read admit that the writer is not occupied in giving legal, financial, medical, or other advice. We put this book content by sourcing various places.

Please consult a licensed professional before you try any techniques shown in this book. By going through this document, the book lover comes to an agreement that under no situation is the author accountable for any forfeiture, direct or indirect, which they may incur because of the use of material contained in this document, including, but not limited to, — errors, omissions, or inaccuracies.

Travel Around The World Coloring Book

This book belongs to

TanitaTatiana

Color Test Page

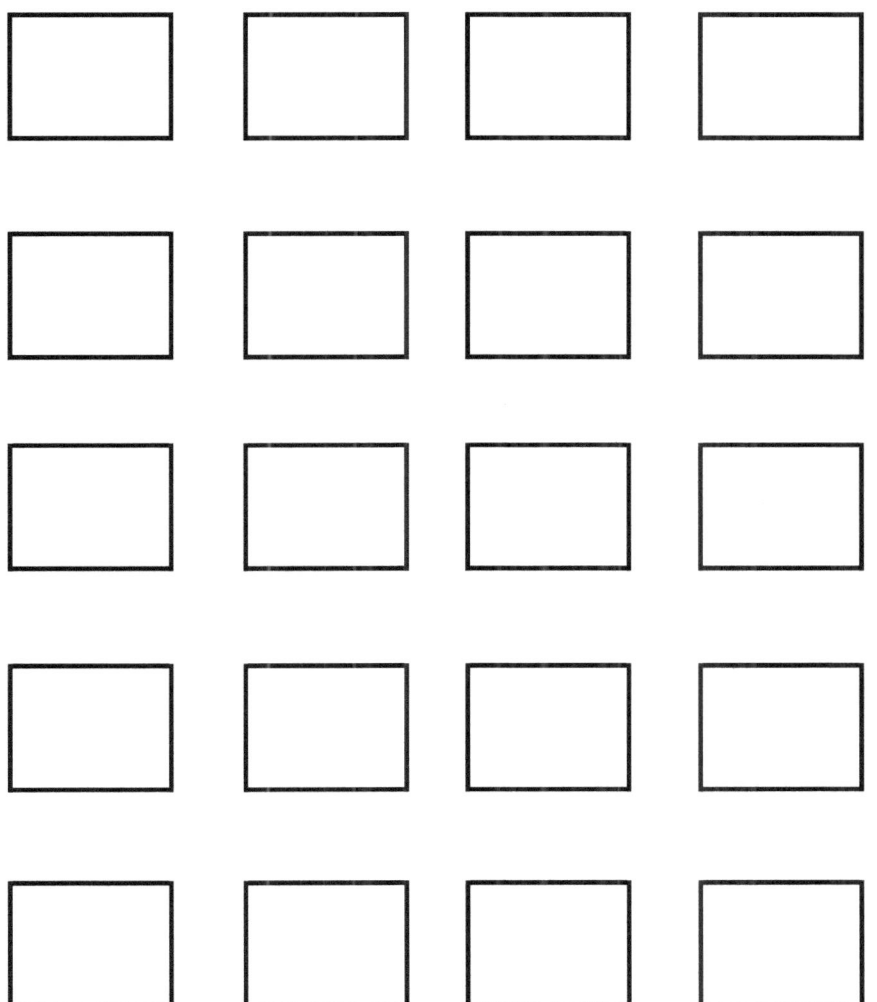

creativity page

Europe

Albania - Capital Tirana
Clock Tower 1822

creativity page

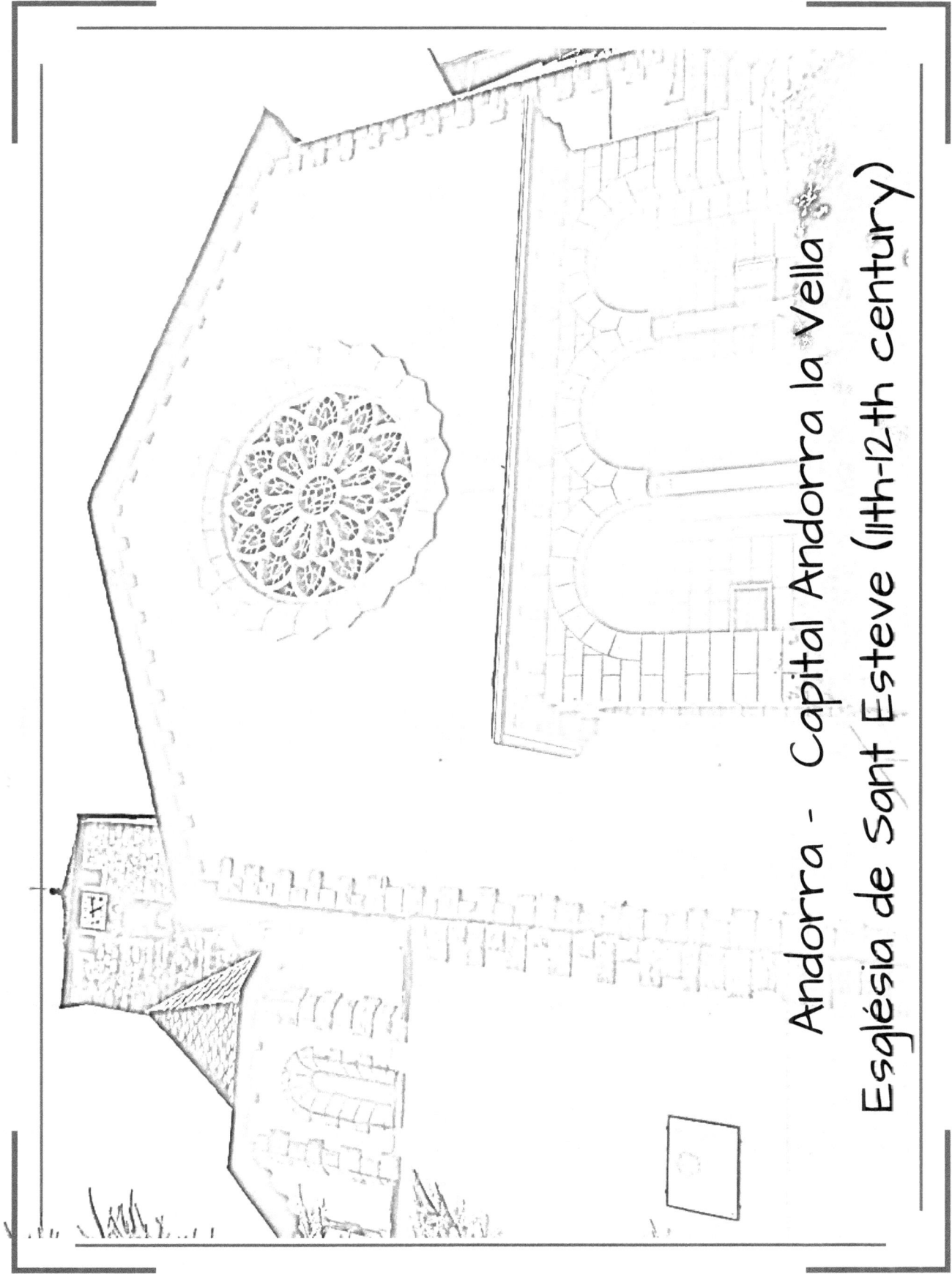

Andorra - Capital Andorra la Vella
Església de Sant Esteve (11th-12th century)

creativity page

creativity page

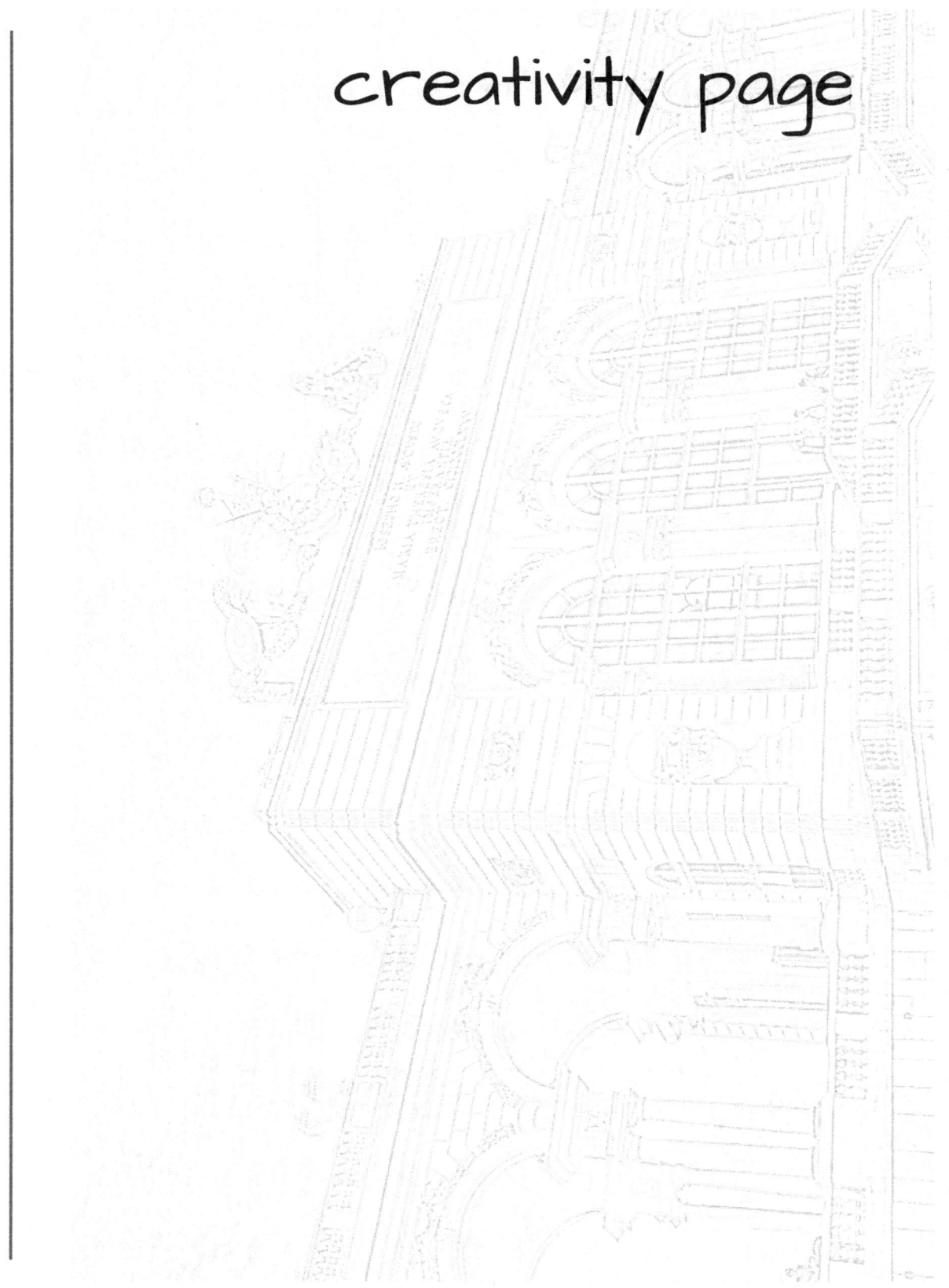

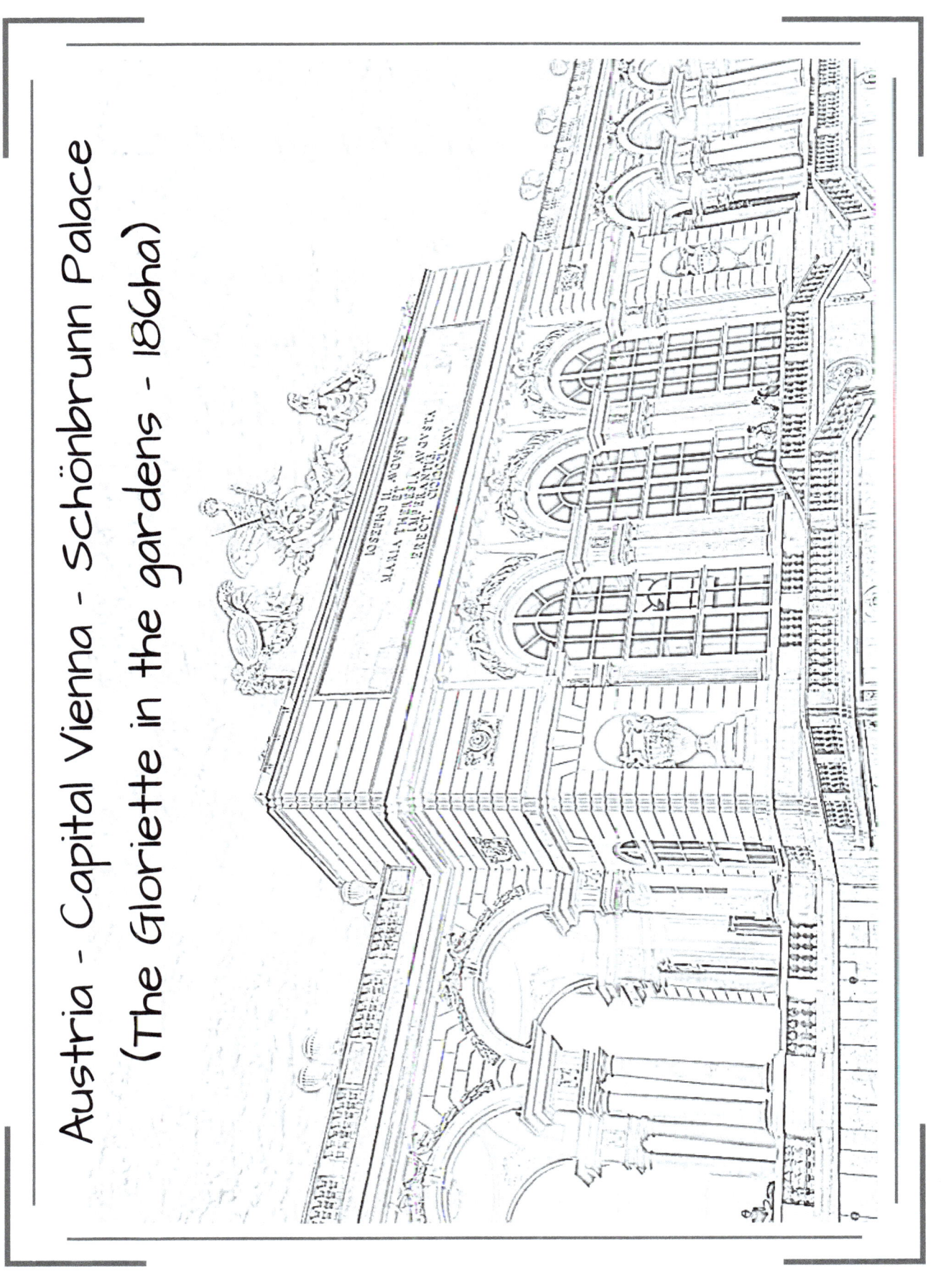

Austria - Capital Vienna - Schönbrunn Palace
(The Gloriette in the gardens - 186ha)

creativity page

Azerbaijan - Capital Baku - Heydar Aliyev Center 2012

creativity page

Belarus - Capital Minsk Church of Saints Simon and Helena (Red Church 1910)

creativity page

Belgium - Capital City of Brussels - Atomium 102m, 1958

creativity page

Bosnia and Herzegovina - Capital
Sarajevo - Gazi Husrev-beg Mosque 26m

creativity page

Bulgaria - Capital Sofia - Alexander Nevsky Cathedral 53m, 1912

creativity page

Croatia - Capital Zagreb - Mimara Museum 1987

creativity page

Cyprus - Capital Nicosia - Liberty Monument 1973

creativity page

creativity page

Denmark - Capital Copenhagen - Windmill at Kastellet 1664

creativity page

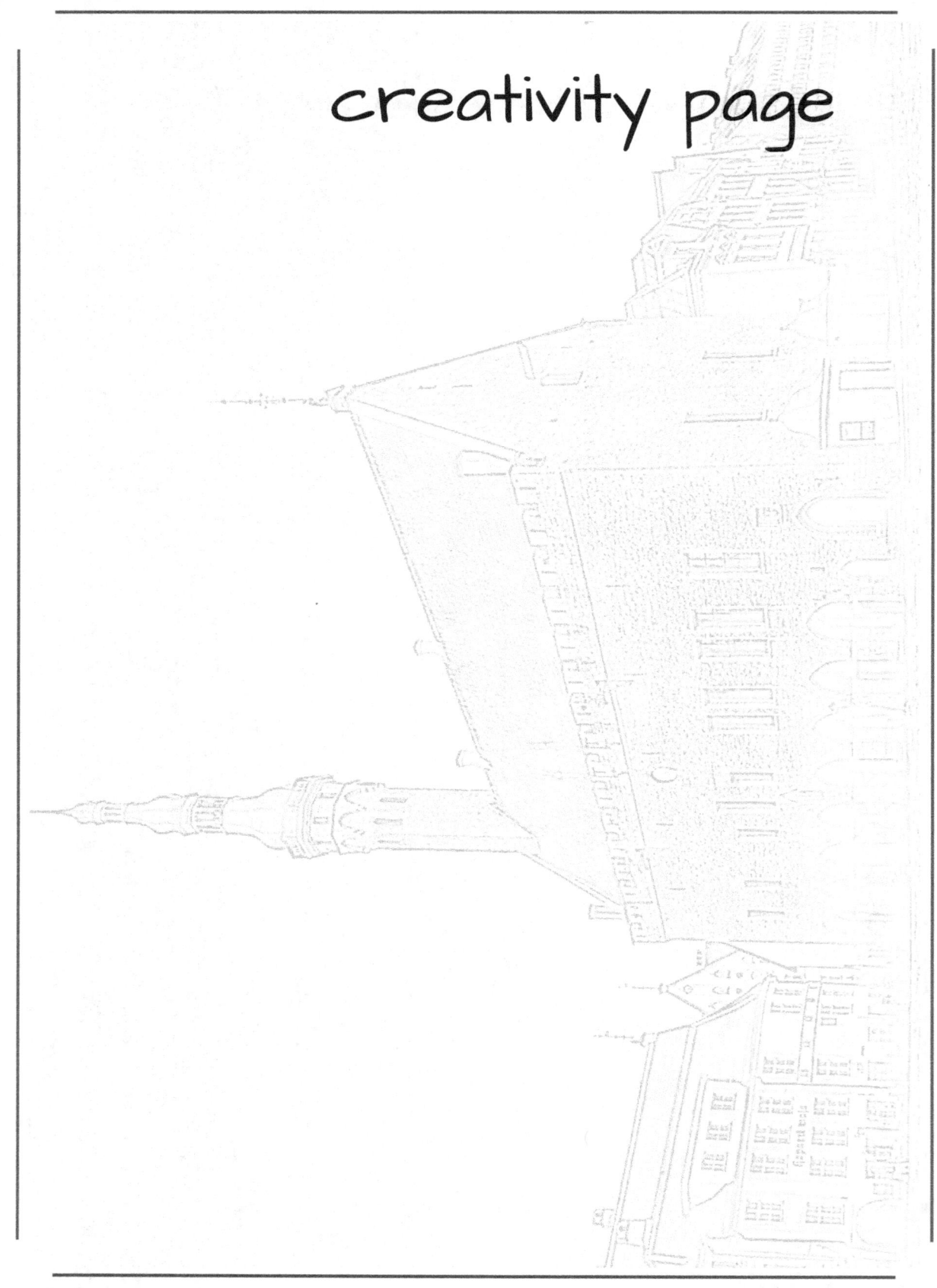

Estonia - Capital Tallinn - Town Hall 1404

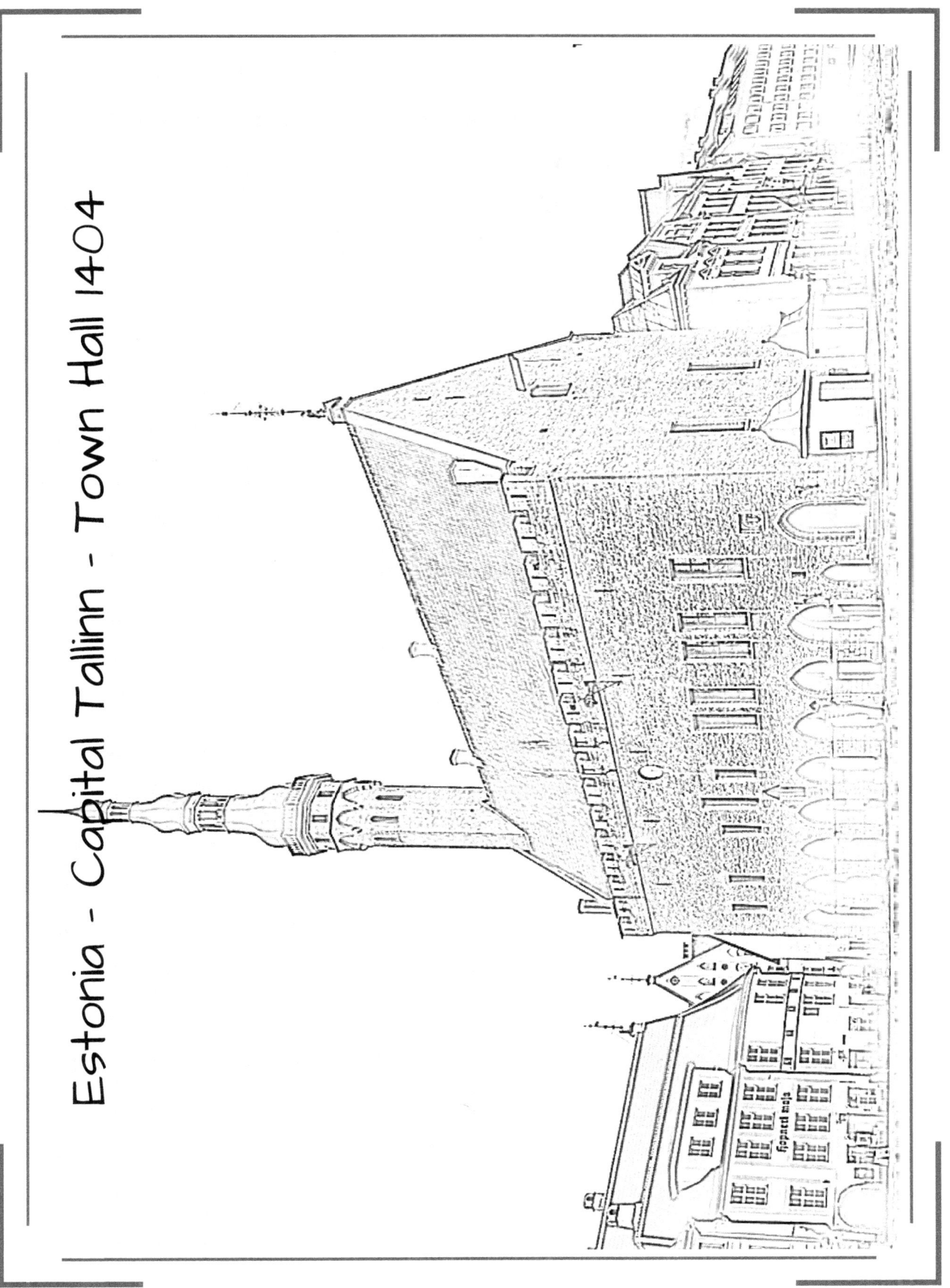

creativity page

Finland - Capital Helsinki - SkyWheel 40m, 2014

creativity page

Georgia - Capital Tbilisi - Freedom Monument
(Saint George and the Dragon 35m 2006)

creativity page

Germany - Capital Berlin - Brandenburg Gate 1791

creativity page

Greece - Capital Athens - Parthenon 432 BC

creativity page

Hungary - Capital Budapest - Liberty Bridge
333.6m, 1896

creativity page

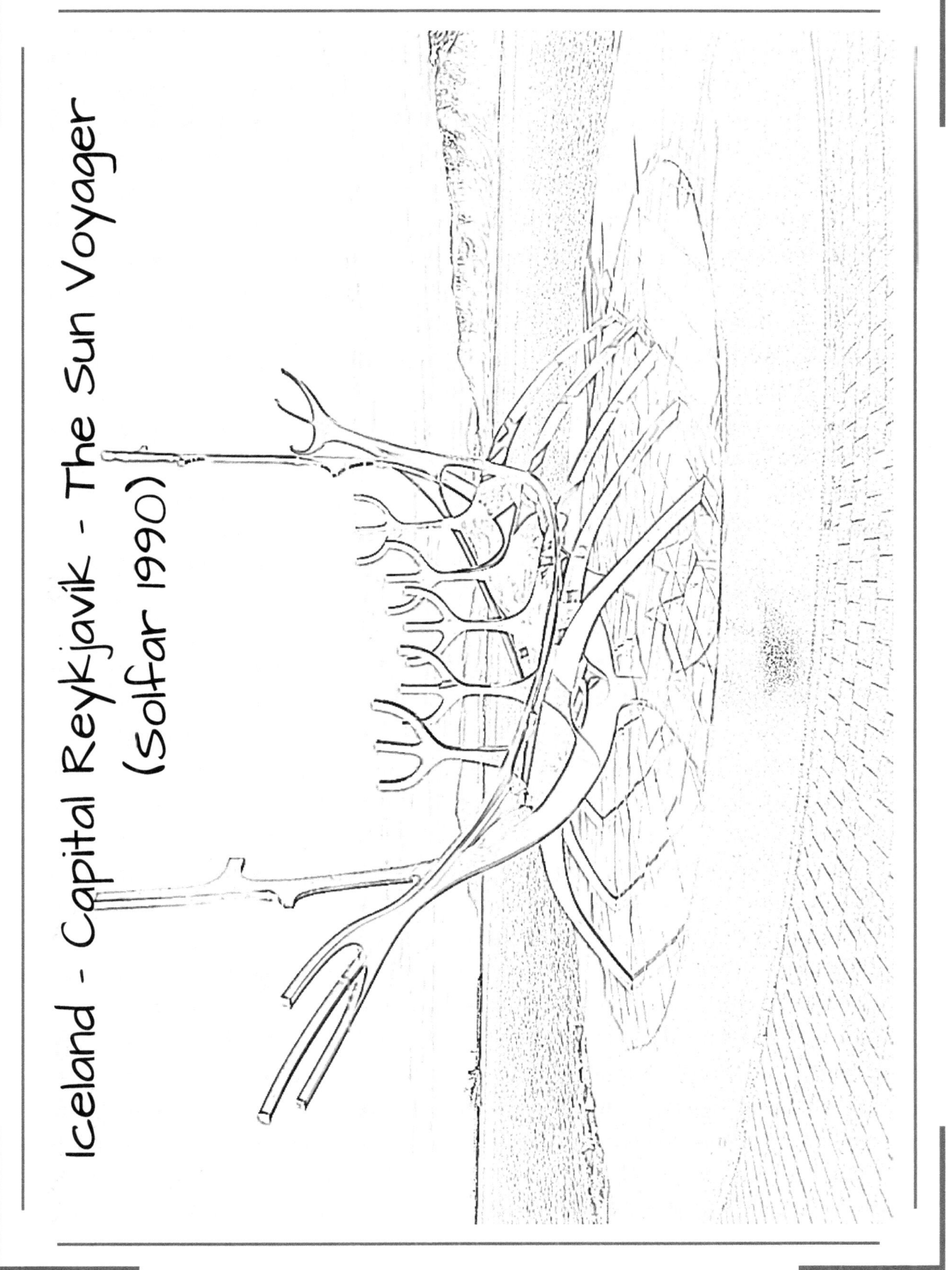
Iceland - Capital Reykjavik - The Sun Voyager (Solfar 1990)

creativity page

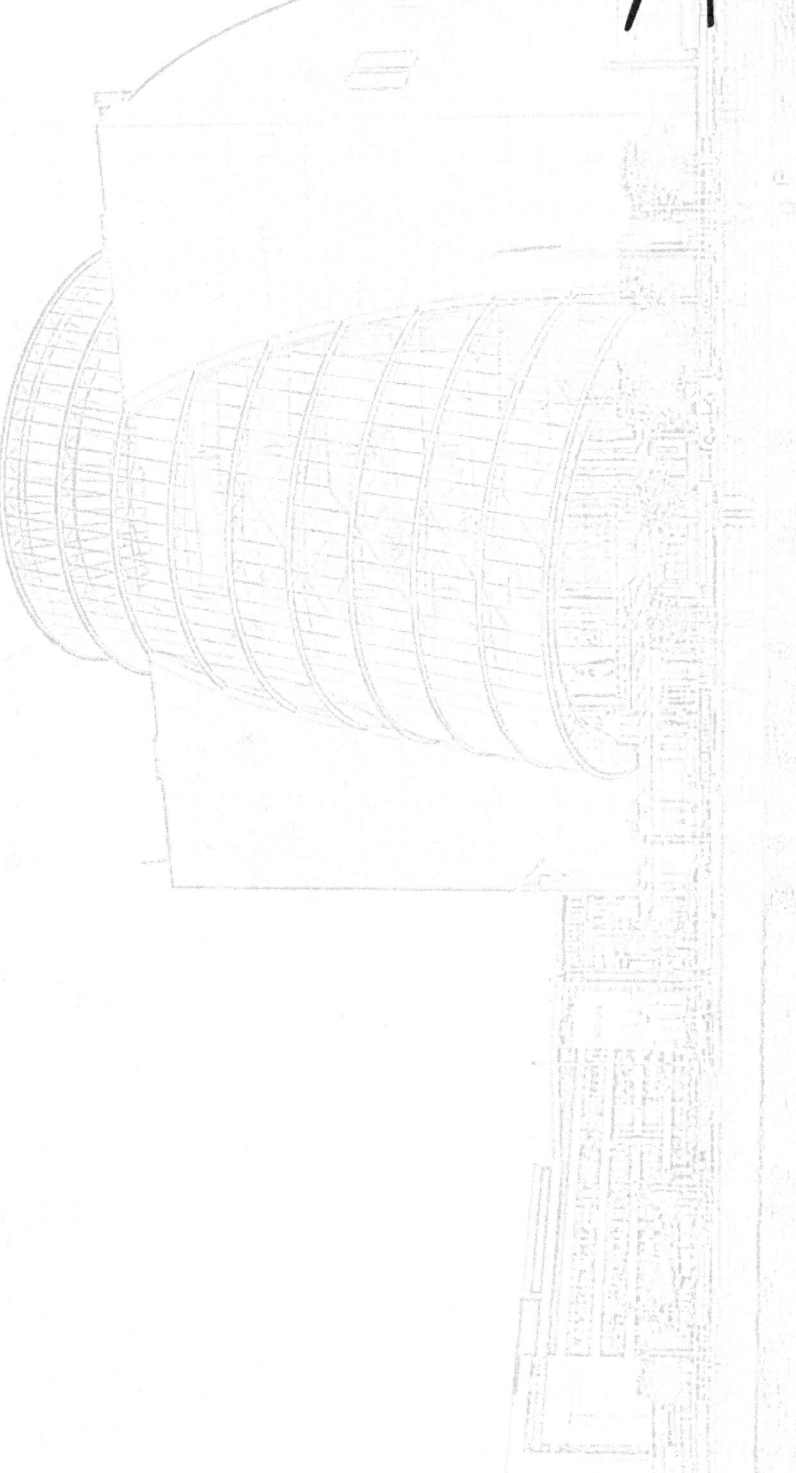

Republic of Ireland - Capital Dublin - Convention Centre 2010

creativity page

Italy - Capital Roma - Colosseum is the largest ancient amphitheater in the world 70-80 AD

creativity page

creativity page

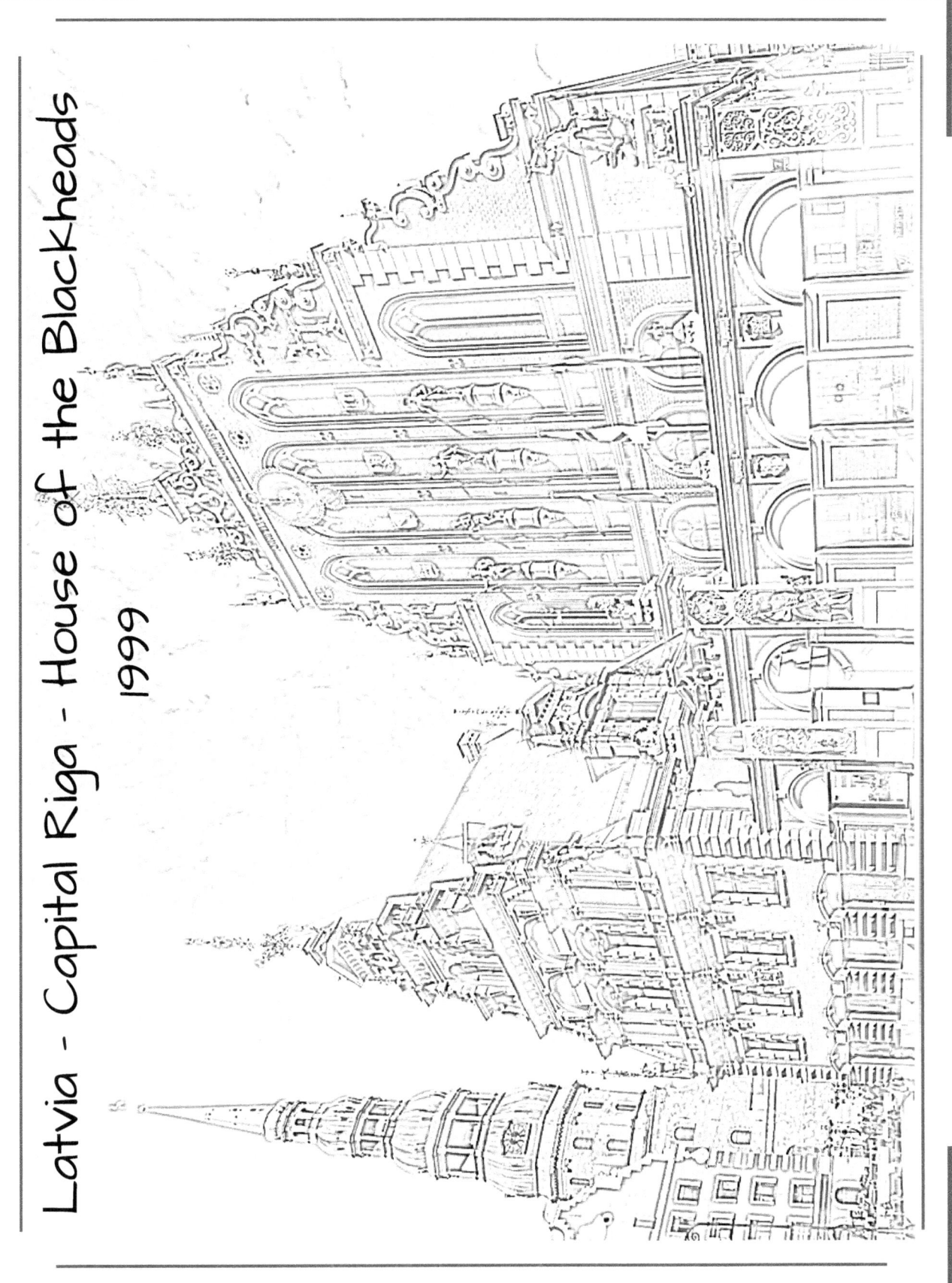

Latvia - Capital Riga - House of the Blackheads
1999

creativity page

Liechtenstein - Capital Vaduz - Landtag (Seats 25 councillors)

creativity page

Lithuania - Capital Vilnius - Gediminas' Tower 1409

creativity page

Luxembourg - Capital Luxembourg City - City Hall

1838

creativity page

Malta - Capital Valletta - Fortifications of Valletta
1566-1570s

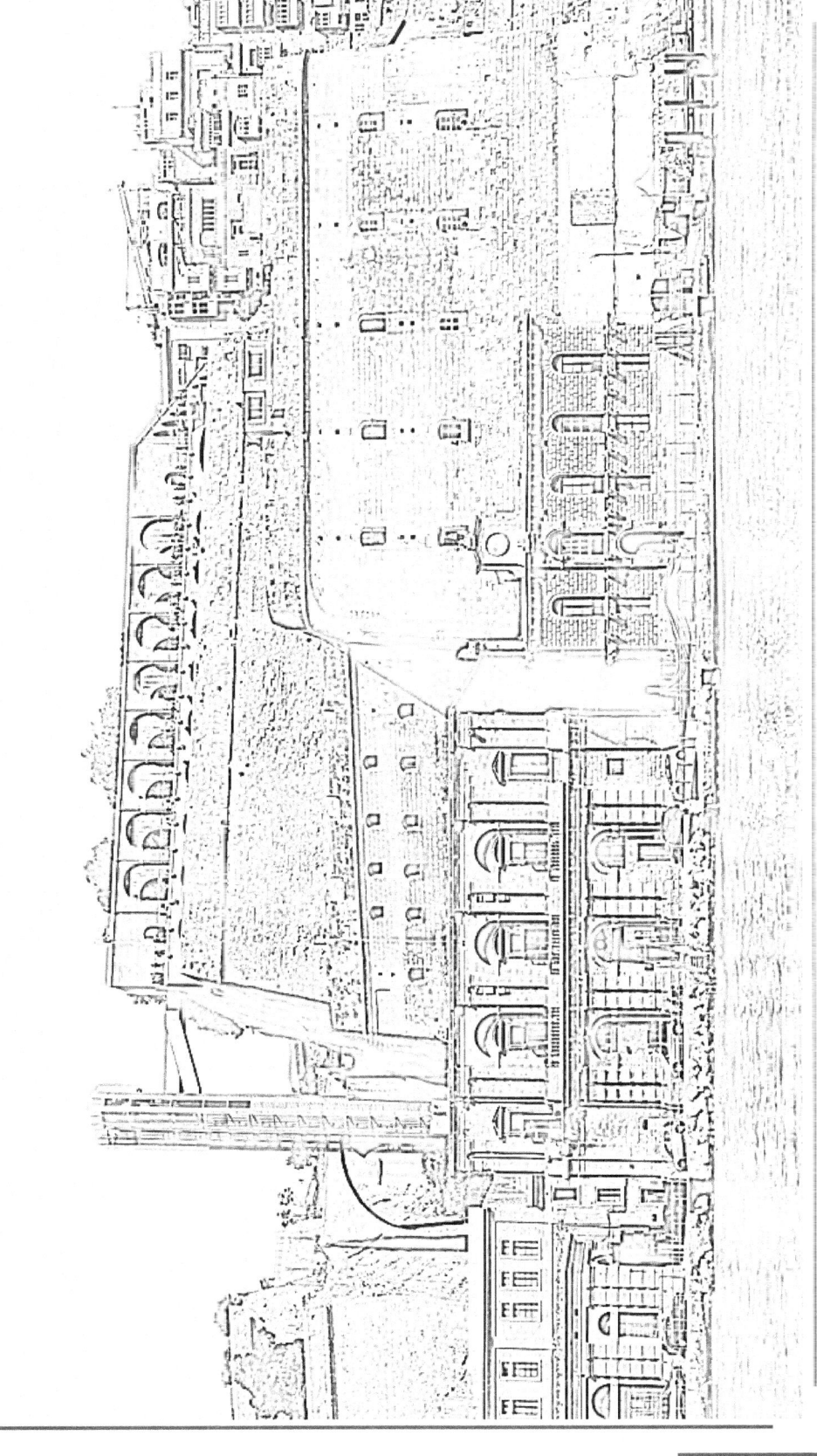

creativity page

Moldova - Capital Chișinău - Triumphal Arch 13m, 1840

creativity page

Monaco - Capital Monaco - Prince's Palace of Monaco 1191

creativity page

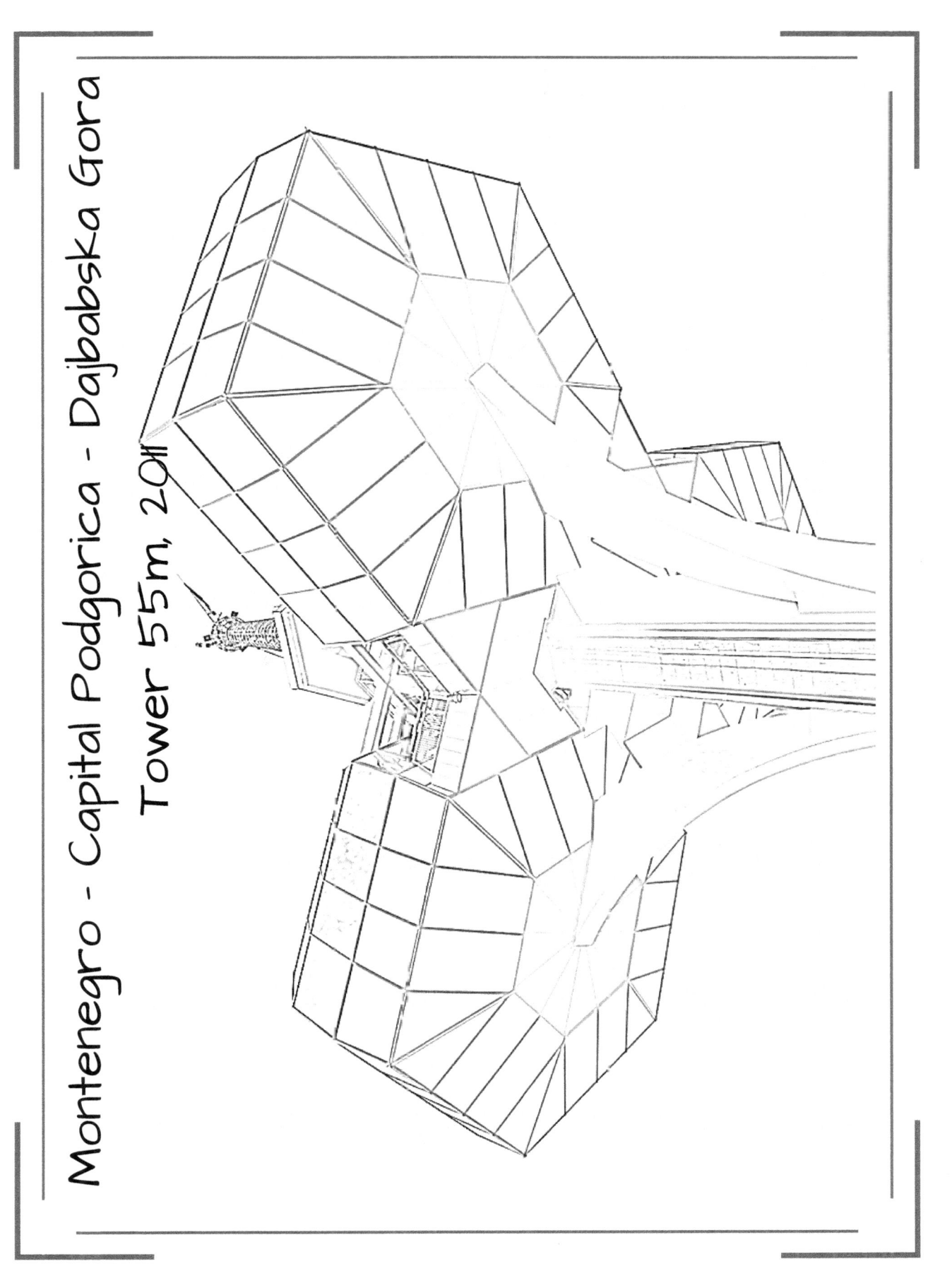

Montenegro - Capital Podgorica - Dajbabska Gora
Tower 55m, 2011

creativity page

Netherlands - Capital Amsterdam - Van Gogh Museum 1973

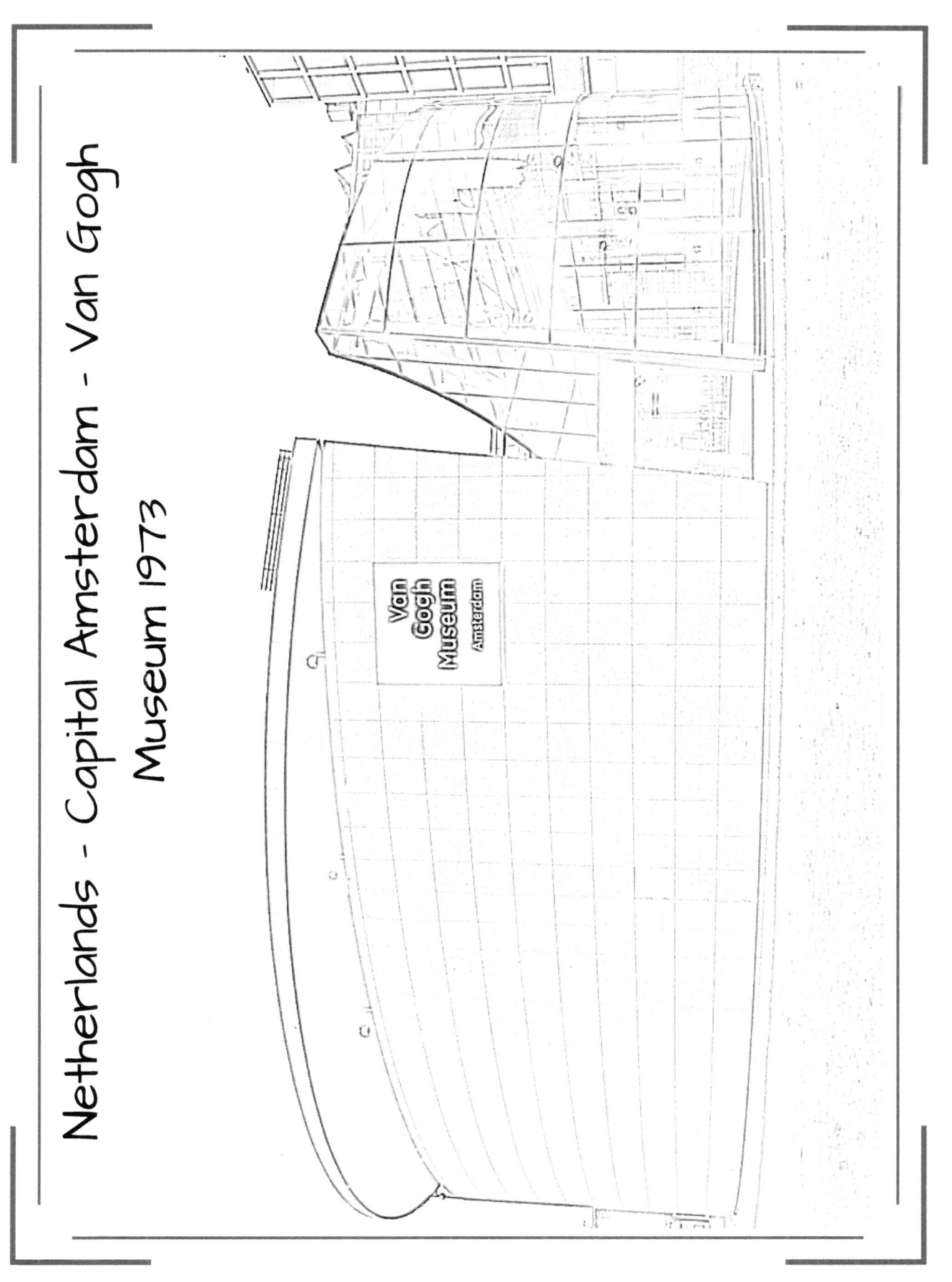

creativity page

North Macedonia - Capital Skopje - Alexander the Great 24m, 2011

creativity page

Norway - Capital Oslo - The Holmenkollen Ski Jump
134m, 1892

creativity page

Poland - Capital Warsaw - Staszic Palace and Nicolaus Copernicus Monument 1830

creativity page

creativity page

Romania - Capital Bucharest - People's House (the heaviest building in the world - 4.10 million tonnes)

creativity page

Russia - Capital Moscow - Saint Basil's Cathedral 1561

creativity page

San Marino - Capital City of San Marino - Palazzo Pubblico 1894

creativity page

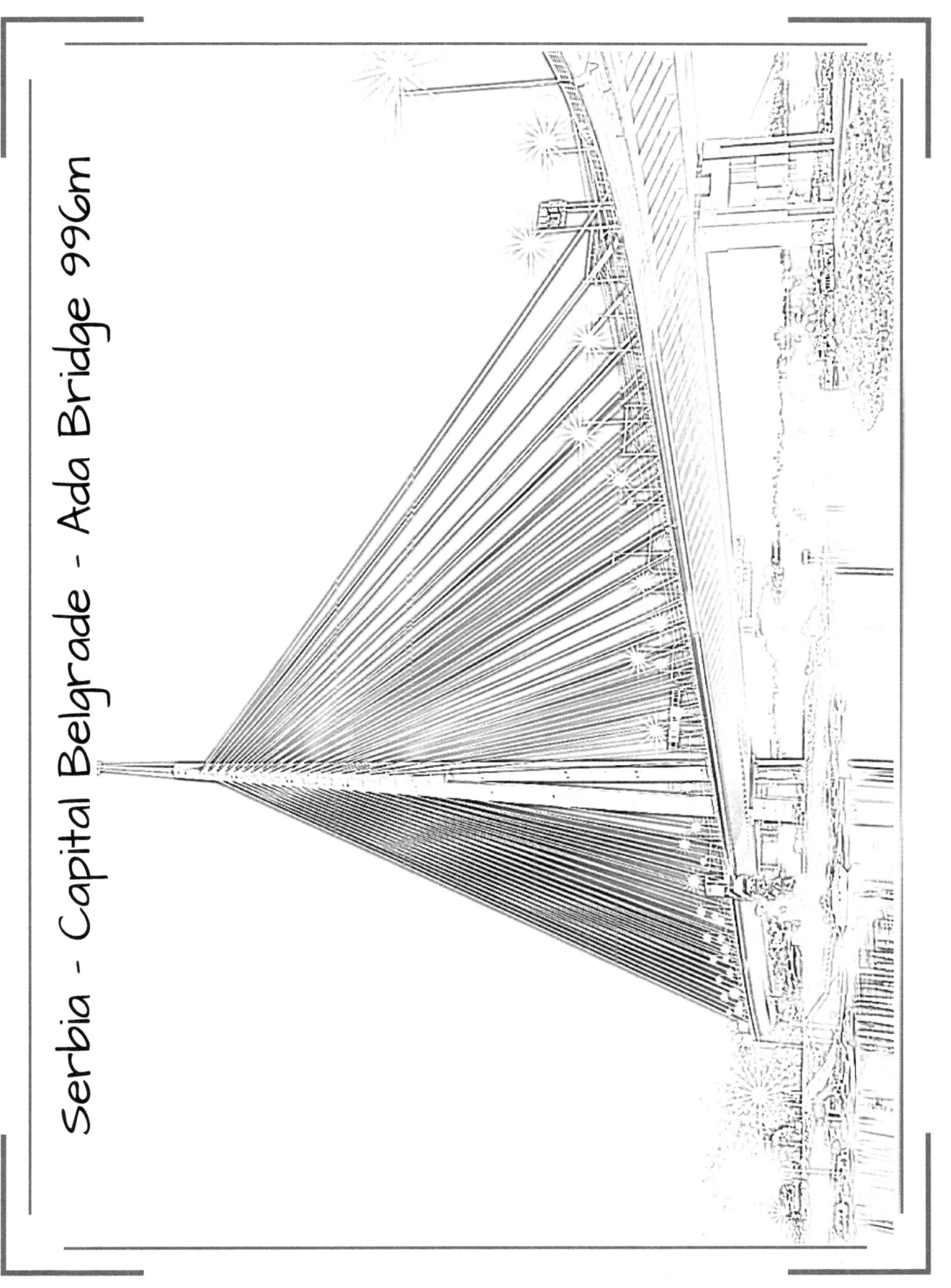

Serbia - Capital Belgrade - Ada Bridge 996m

creativity page

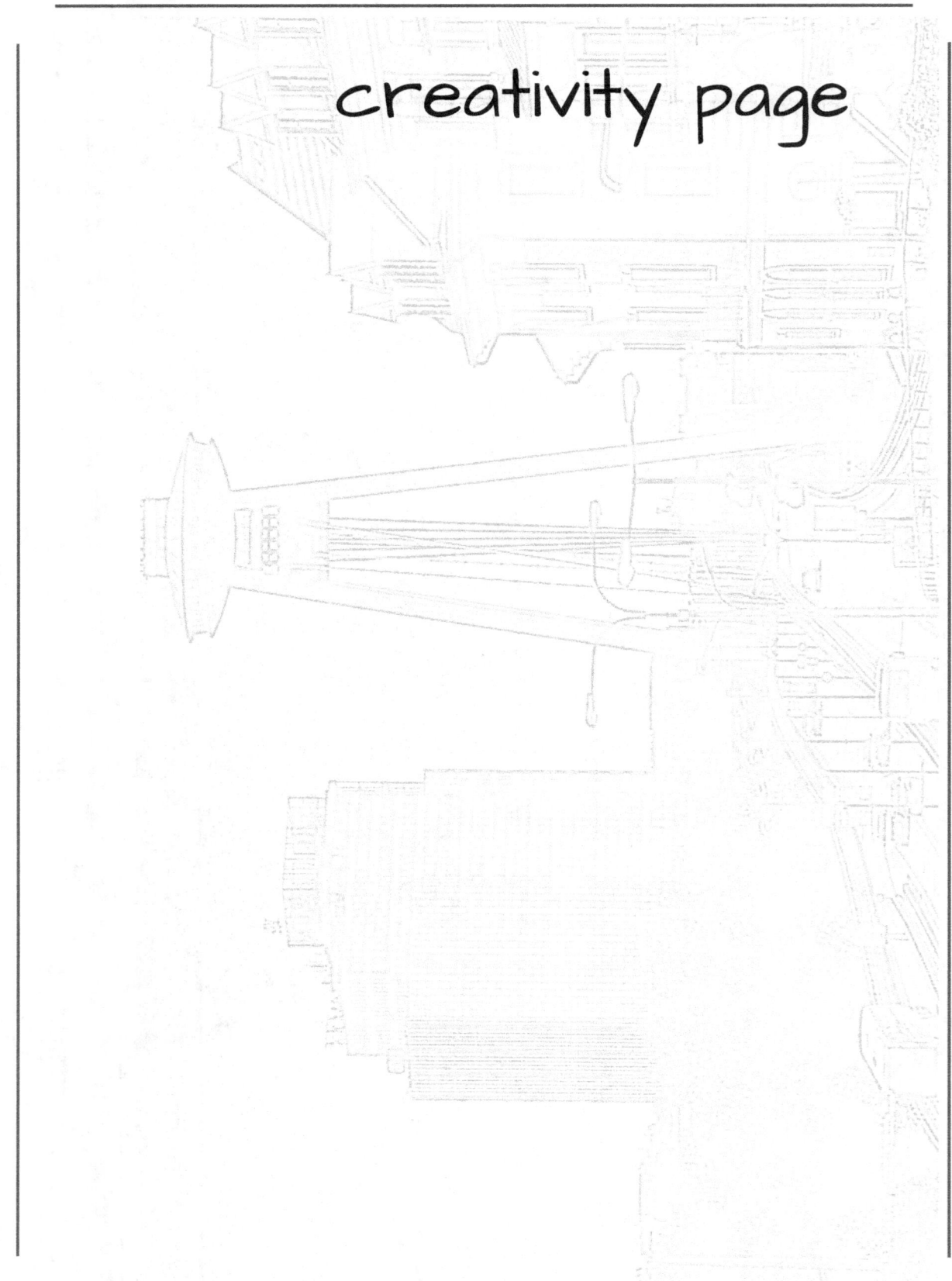

Slovakia - Capital Bratislava - UFO Observation Deck

95m

creativity page

Spain - Capital Madrid - Puerta de Alcalá 1778

creativity page

Sweden - Capital Stockholm - The Ericsson Globe is the largest hemispherical building on Earth (diameter of 110m)

creativity page

Switzerland - Capital Bern (de facto - federal city) - Zentrum Paul Klee Museum 2005

creativity page

Turkey - Capital Ankara - Kocatepe Mosque 1987

creativity page

Ukraine - Capital Kyiv - Independence Monument (Statue of Berehynia - 61m)

creativity page

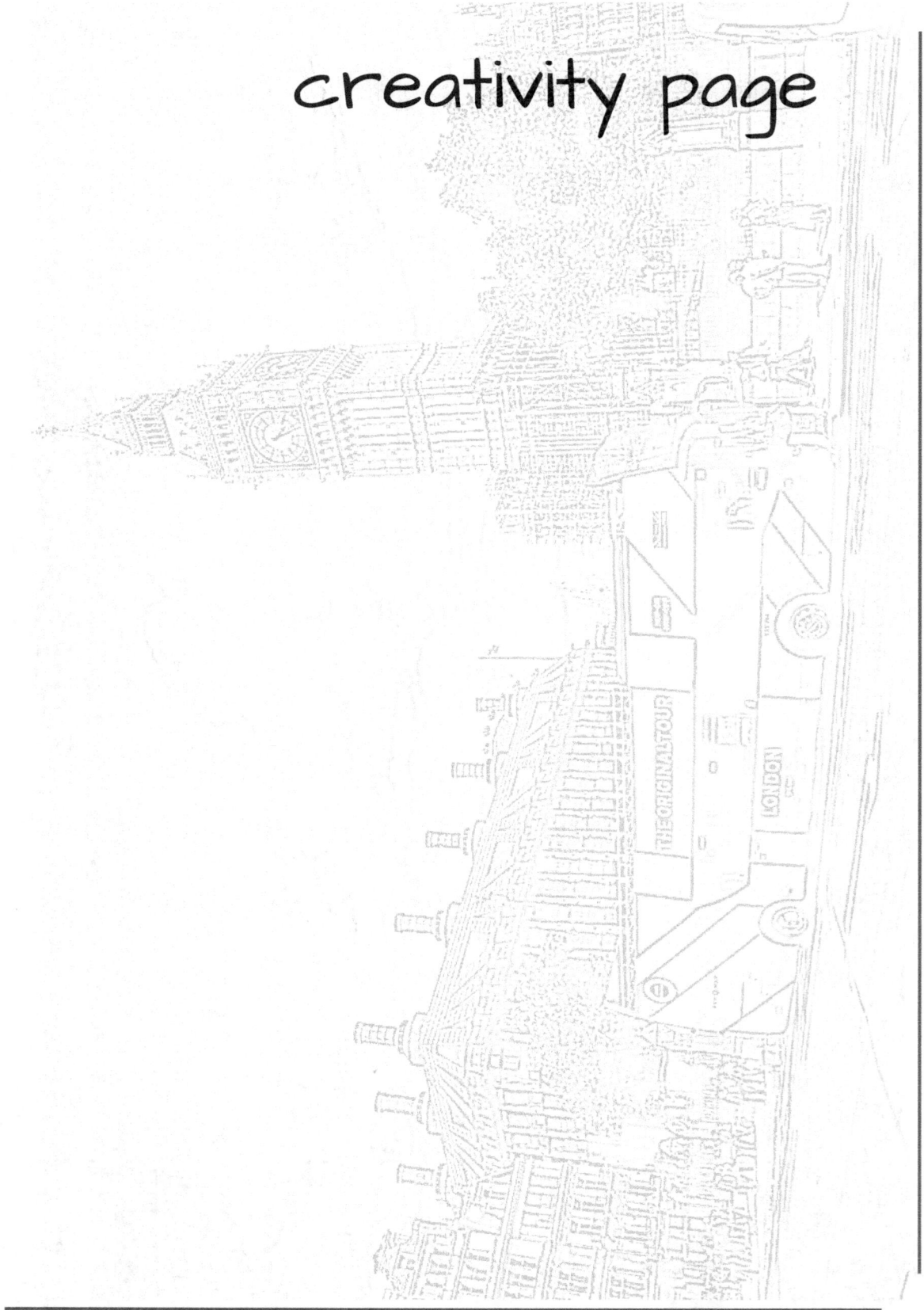

United Kingdom - Capital London - Big Ben 96m, 1859

creativity page

Vatican City - Capital Vatican City - St. Peter's Basilica 1626

creativity page

Thank you.

We hope you enjoyed our book.

As a small family company, your feedback is very important to us.

Please let us know how you like our book at:

tanitatatiana04@gmail.com

www.ingramcontent.com/pod-product-compliance
Lightning Source LLC
LaVergne TN
LVHW081539060526
838200LV00048B/2150